Written by Sue Graves
Illustrated by Jacqueline East
Designed by Blue Sunflower Creative

Language consultant: Betty Root

This is a Parragon book
First published in 2003

Parragon
Queen Street House
4 Queen Street
Bath, BA1 1HE, UK

ISBN 1-40542-199-1
Printed in China

What a Bad Goat!

A Level 1 Reading Book

p

Notes for Parents

Reading with your child is an enjoyable and rewarding experience. These **Gold Stars** reading books encourage and support children who are learning to read.

There are four different levels of reading book in the series. Within each level, the books can be read in any order. The steps between the levels are deliberately small because it is so important at this early stage for children to succeed. Success creates confidence.

Starting to read

Start by reading the book aloud to your child, taking time to talk about the pictures. This will help your child to see that pictures often give clues about the story.

Over a period of time, try to read the same book several times so that your child becomes familiar with the story and the words and phrases. Then your child will be ready to read the book aloud with you. It helps to run your finger under the words as you say them.

Occasionally, stop and encourage your child to continue reading aloud without you. Join in again when your child needs help. This is the next step towards helping your child become an independent reader.

Finally, your child will be ready to read alone. Listen carefully to your child and give plenty of praise. Remember to make reading an enjoyable experience.

Using your Gold Stars stickers

You can use the **Gold Stars** stickers at the back of the book as a reward for effort as well as achievement. Learning to read is an exciting challenge for every child.

Remember these four important stages:

- Read the story **to** your child.
- Read the story **with** your child.
- Encourage your child to read **to you**.
- Listen to your child read **alone**.

Here is Farmer Jim.

Farmer Jim is going to
see his animals.

Pig is looking after
her piglets.

"What a good pig!" says Farmer Jim.

Hen is laying an egg.

"What a good hen!" says
Farmer Jim.

13

Horse is eating some hay.

"What a good horse!" says
Farmer Jim.

Cow is giving lots of milk.

"What a good cow!" says
Farmer Jim.

17

Sheep is feeding her lambs.

"What a good sheep!" says
Farmer Jim.

Duck is teaching her ducklings to swim.

"What a good duck!" says
Farmer Jim.

Cat is chasing mice from
the barn.

"What a good cat!" says
Farmer Jim.

Dog is looking after
the house.

"What a good dog!" says
Farmer Jim.

But Goat is eating the washing.

"Oh, what a bad goat!"
says Farmer Jim.

27

Look back in your book.
Can you find these words?

pig

duck

sheep

cat

dog

goat

Gold Stars

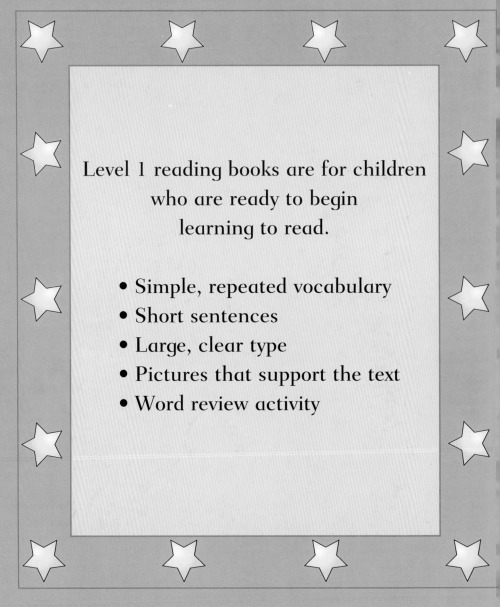

Level 1 reading books are for children
who are ready to begin
learning to read.

- Simple, repeated vocabulary
- Short sentences
- Large, clear type
- Pictures that support the text
- Word review activity